THE RISING
HERE COME THE KINGS AND PRIESTS

BY DICK BERNAL

THE RISING – HERE COME THE KINGS AND PRIESTS
COPYRIGHT © 2013 DICK BERNAL

ISBN 978-1884920073

Originally published A COMMUNITY OF KINGS & PRIESTS © 2007 (ISBN 1-884920-25-x

JUBILEE CHRISTIAN CENTER PUBLICATION
175 Nortech Parkway
San Jose, California 95134
www.jubilee.org

PRINTED IN THE UNITED STATES OF AMERICA

THE RISING
HERE COME THE KINGS AND PRIESTS

TABLE OF CONTENTS

THE RISING
HERE COME THE KINGS AND PRIESTS

ACKNOWLEDGMENTS

I would like to thank Pastor Charles Neiman of El Paso, Texas, for sparking this revelation in my heart and mind nearly twenty years ago. – **Pastor Dick Bernal, Senior Pastor, Jubilee Christian Center**

There is an equilibrium that is imperative to making great strides of success in the Kingdom of God and in business. Pastor Dick Bernal is equipped with the education and experience in these arenas to offer the greatest insight concerning this matter. It is all revealed in his new book, "The Rising – Here Come the Kings and Priests. – **Pastor Rick Hawkins, Sr. Pastor, Place For Life, San Antonio, Texas**

Pastor Bernal's insight on Kings and Priests brings Biblical clarity and revelation that translates into empowerment to every Christ-follower who embraces the content on the pages of this great book! Pastor Bernal's years of ministry in the marketplace and from his pulpit at Jubilee Christian Center, one of America's great churches, as well as his influence in the body of Christ around the world uniquely qualifies him to speak on this most important subject. I strongly recommend to every Christian to extract the spiritual nourishment that lies in the pages of The Rising – Here Come The Kings and Priests. Prepare for elevation! – **Pastor Steve Hage, Sr. Pastor, The Gathering Community Church, Laguna Niguel, California**

FOREWORD

In Dick Bernal's powerful book, The Rising (Here Come the Kings and Priests), he unearths the real meaning of the normal Christian life and teaches us how to walk in our divine mandate as Kings and Priests. Kings are those who work full time in the marketplace, and Priests are people who serve in the ministry. It is a clarion call to men and women to rise up as powerful, supernatural, wonder working business people and to make disciples of all nations.

For much of church history, we have assumed that to be "in the ministry" meant working for a church. The anointed ones were full-time pastors, while those who worked "in the world" were just not quite as spiritual. Even though the church makes a distinction between the two, the Bible does not.

We seem to have lost sight of the fact that the ministry that we are called to emulate was a counterculture revolutionary who walked in supernatural power. He lived, died, and rose again to deliver an ailing planet from the power of the devil and to extend the Superior Kingdom into every corner of the planet. The only way we can accomplish this is if our Christian men and women have a clear understanding of their calling, anointing and focus and that they see their careers as their primary expression for building God's kingdom.

It's very possible that Dick Bernal's book could equip marketplace Christians to become spiritual and natural leaders, establishing the Kingdom of God in every sphere of influence. If you are longing to get equipped with supernatural power in order to see societies transformed, then this book is for you!

Kris Vallotton
Leader, Bethel Church, Redding, CA
Co-Founder of Bethel School of Supernatural Ministry
Author of nine books including, The Supernatural Ways of Royalty and Spirit Wars

INTRODUCTION

Arise, shine; for your light has come!
And the glory of the Lord is risen upon you.
For behold, the darkness shall cover the earth,
And deep darkness the people; But the Lord
will arise over you, and His glory will- be seen
upon you. The Gentiles shall come to your light,
And kings to the brightness of your rising.
"Lift up your eyes all around, and see: They all
gather together, they come to you; your sons shall
come from afar, and your daughters shall be
nursed at your side. Then you shall see and
become radiant, and your heart shall swell with
joy; because the abundance of the sea shall be
turned to you, the wealth of the Gentiles shall
come to you. The multitude of camels shall cover
your land, the dromedaries of Midian and
Ephah; all those from Sheba shall come;
They shall bring gold and incense, and they shall
proclaim the praises of the Lord. All the flocks of
Kedar shall be gathered together to you, the
rams of Nebaioth shall minister to you; they
shall ascend with acceptance on My altar, and I
will glorify the house of My glory. "Who are these
who fly like a cloud, and like doves to their roosts?
- Isaiah 60:1-3

Isaiah saw the coming brightness, light and largeness to Zion and to

the House of the Lord. This of course began when Christ came and

brought "light" with Him. We might simply call it illumination,

revelation of the knowledge of God and His plan for man.

Perhaps Isaiah got a peek at 1948, the return of God's ancient people to their homeland where once again the "desert would bloom" but, whether Isaiah was cognizant or not, the Holy Spirit used him to prophesy about these present and very near days. The glorious, attractive church of our Lord Jesus Christ will become this undeniable magnet pulling people into the Kingdom from every walk of life.

Children, parents, siblings, the rich, the famous, the powerful, the influential, etc. will all find their way home to God, like Solomon, who somehow found his place of origin even through extremely difficult circumstances.

Isaiah also saw unprecedented wealth coming to the House of the Lord for the plain and simple purpose of "honor". This revival will first bring fear and uncertainty, but soon will give way to joy and excitement. As clouds can gather seemingly out of nowhere, and droves of doves can quickly swoop in and cover a roof, or tree or even a window, so will the multitudes come from near and far to God's House.

Obviously we in leadership will be caught somewhat off guard. Isaiah saw it – the massive crowds, the financial blessings, the prominent humbly worshipping God with the poor and hurting. Let's pick up in Isaiah 60:15-22:

> "Whereas you have been forsaken and hated,
> So that no one went through you, I will make you

an eternal excellence, A joy of many generations. You shall drink the milk of the Gentiles, and milk the breast of kings; You shall know that I, the Lord, am your Savior and your Redeemer, the Mighty One of Jacob. "Instead of bronze I will bring gold, Instead of iron I will bring silver, Instead of wood, bronze, and instead of stones, iron. I will also make your officers peace, and your magistrates righteousness. Violence shall no longer be heard in your land, neither wasting nor destruction within your borders; But you shall call your walls Salvation, And your gates Praise. God the Glory of His People "The sun shall no longer be your light by day, nor for brightness shall the moon give light to you; but the Lord will be to you an everlasting light, and your God your glory. Your sun shall no longer go down, nor shall your moon withdraw itself; for the Lord will be your everlasting light, and the days of your mourning shall be ended. Also your people shall all be righteous; they shall inherit the land forever, the branch of My planting, the work of My hands, that I may be glorified. A little one shall become a thousand, and a small one a strong nation. I, the Lord, will hasten it in its time."

As a Pastor who has been pastoring for thirty-three years, all I can say is, "Wow!" I want to live long enough to see this!

Even our poor, small, despised churches will have an awesome breakthrough. Crime will abate, poverty will cease, laughter will replace mourning, and peace will rule one's soul. Come on, Jesus! We are ready!

The last verse (22) tells us, "The little ones will become a thousand, and small ones, a strong nation." Little churches will explode; bigger, larger ones will look like a small nation. Mega churches will become commonplace.

Notice, "I, the Lord, will hasten it." Amos saw it this way:

> "Behold, the days are coming," says the Lord,
> "When the plowman shall overtake the reaper,
> And the treader of grapes him who sows seed;
> The mountains shall drip with sweet wine, And all
> the hills shall flow with it. I will bring back the
> captives of My people Israel; They shall build the
> waste cities and inhabit them; They shall plant
> vineyards and drink wine from them; They shall
> also make gardens and eat fruit from them.
> - Amos 9:13-14

Accelerated harvest! For those of us who believe this can really happen, how do we plan, pray and prepare? That's the purpose of this book, *The Rising*. Peter told us, "make our calling and election sure." Every believer is called, anointed, and appointed, but to what? My prayer is that *The Rising* will help you "make sure" your "gift" is clear and your "call" productive.

CHAPTER 1
THE DISCOVERY

I'm always asking the question: What do you want
to be remembered for? If you are fortunate,
someone with moral authority will ask you that
question early enough in your life so that you will
continue to ask it as you go through life. It is a
question that induces you to renew yourself,
because it pushes you to see yourself as a
different person – the person you can become.
- Peter Drucker

William Shakespeare wrote, *"The most important thing for a man or woman to do is to find out who he or she is . . ."* I would add, *"in Christ"*! It's obvious to me with the great success of Rick Warren's book, **"PURPOSE DRIVEN LIFE,"** that people are interested in knowing where they fit in. *"Who am I?" "What am I?" "Where should I be?" "What is my life really all about?"*

Nearly twenty years ago, I was in the Toronto area speaking at a conference for a pastor friend. We were driving to lunch when he asked me if I had ever read the Book of Revelation and wondered why John, decades after the church was birthed, used the titles "Kings and Priests" to describe us believers.

"John, to the seven churches which are in Asia:
Grace to you and peace from Him who is and
who was and who is to come, and from the seven
Spirits who are before His throne, and from Jesus
Christ, the faithful witness, the firstborn from the
dead, and the ruler over the kings of the earth.
To Him who loved us and washed us from our
sins in His own blood, and has made us kings
and priests to His God and Father, to Him be
glory and dominion forever and ever. Amen."
- Revelation 1:4-6

He told me about a visiting speaker, Pastor Charles Neiman from El Paso, Texas, who brought to light a new way of looking at "ministry". Kings, under Jesus the King of Kings, are marketplace ministers. Priests are those who serve God within the five-fold ministry calling that includes Apostle, Prophet, Evangelist, Pastor, and Teacher - as well as those on staff of a ministry called to "helps".

I immediately felt the Holy Spirit stirring, impressing me that there was something He wanted to reveal – a new principle to be understood and taught. Fascinated, I went home and began to search this out, spending hours, days, and months studying. What I discovered, and have been sharing around the world since, has been written on the pages of this book.

GETTING ON THE RIGHT PATH

This message of empowering God's Kings has received its share of criticism. Recently, I was ministering in South America where several hundred pastors gathered to host a "Reyes/Sacrimentos Conference (Kings and Priests). They told me a story that both blessed and surprised me. In 2001 I was in their country speaking at a large gathering and in one of my forty minute sessions, I shared the basics of this teaching. Little did I know it was the polar opposite of what the host pastor thought and enforced rather vigorously. His belief was that if a person was serious about God, they should leave their career, business, or job, and go into "real" ministry and either start a church or become a ministry-supporting staff member. This, of course, kept successful business people and the educated away from church.

During my talk, a few of the frustrated pastors "caught the vision". It took years, but hundreds of churches are now empowering "Kings" to engage in the marketplace with God's calling and anointing to be successful in business and to share the gospel with their "crowd". Of course, I'm not the only one doing this. For years, Ed Silvoso, Rich Marshall, and my old friend and author, Ken Eldred, have shared similar concepts.

My desire and prayer is that, as you begin to understand the distinct individual and collaborative roles of modern day Kings and

Priests, our precious Lord will confirm your role and purpose and quickly get you on the path to fulfilling your mandate!

> "Therefore, brethren, be even more diligent to make your call and election sure, for if you do these things you will never stumble; for so an entrance will be supplied to you abundantly into the everlasting kingdom of our Lord and Savior Jesus Christ."
> - 2 Peter 1:10-11

CHAPTER 2
NEW WINE THINKING

Being successful and fulfilling your life's
purpose are not at all the same things; You
can reach all your personal goals, become a
raving success by the world's standard and
still miss your purpose in this life.
- Rick Warren

WHAT IS THE CHURCH ANYWAY?

In this chapter, I will address what I believe is one of the great injustices in the body of Christ today. When we see someone "on fire" for God, we automatically think they must be called to the ministry and put them in our ministry box. We interpret *"called"* as *"the ministry"*. Of course ministry to us means working in or for the church. Therefore, we believe the proper path for a called person begins with Bible School followed by an assignment to some type of post in a church. We applaud their zeal and pray for their success.

The rest of us go about our secular work routine and do our best to attend church, give, sing, listen, maybe volunteer, and fellowship - all the while thinking that the serious part of church is what goes on up on the platform with the *"anointed"* or "called" servants of God. We still think *"church"* is a building and what takes place on Sunday mornings is our time to worship. The rest of the week we go about our lives and try our best not to get too "worldly".

When we examine the differences in the Old and New Testaments, we see both covenants described "Kings" who ruled and "Priests" who ministered to God. However, with the emergence of the New Testament church, we see the use of other terms such as, elders, deacons, bishops, overseers, and handmaidens. The church is an "ecclesia", a Greek word meaning "called out for military or political service."

In Jesus's day, the building where people attended church was called the temple. When Jesus used the term "church" in Matthew 16:18 – *"And I also say to you that you are Peter, and on this rock I will build My church, and the gates of hell shall not prevail against it."* – He was not talking about the temple or a building. He was speaking about "ecclesia" – the body of Christ.

So, you see, we all fit into this category whether we are employed by the church or a part of the body of Christ, attending and serving, but employed outside the church. We are the church.

By God's grace I am going to do my best to renew our minds through the principles of this book. It is essential we use "Kingdom thinking" which says every Christian is "called, anointed, and appointed" to do something to help build the Kingdom, whether in the marketplace or in the five-fold ministry, and all should work together to build the Kingdom.

> These things I have written to you concerning those who try to deceive you. But the anointing which you have received from Him abides in you, and you do not need that anyone teach you; but as the same anointing teaches you concerning all things, and is true, and is not a lie, and just as it has taught you, you will abide in Him.
> - 1 John 2:26-27

MINISTER OR MARKETPLACE?

By definition, a minister is someone who is authorized by a church or religious organization to perform functions such as teaching of beliefs, leading weddings, baptisms or funerals, and otherwise providing spiritual guidance to the community. The term is taken from the Latin word (actually spelled the same) minister meaning "servant, attendant", which itself was derived from "minus less." The role, training, and required qualifications vary depending on denomination but a universal belief and standard for a minister is that he or she must sense "a calling".

> Now all things [are] of God, who has reconciled us to Himself through Jesus Christ, and has given us the ministry of reconciliation.
> - 2 Corinthians 5:18

Being a minister of reconciliation is not limited to pulpit ministry. As people who are called to be salt and light to the world, we must recognize we are all called to be ministers of reconciliation. Some of you may have questioned yourself or God by wondering if you can love God and be on fire for Him and yet still love business. *Yes!* Is it okay to love your "secular" job? *Yes!* Is it okay to desire to work in the political realm? *Yes!* Am I being ungodly by desiring to be a professional athlete or Hollywood entertainer? *No!* How else will the world know Jesus Christ and understand God's Kingdom if we are not amongst the world? Every culture and society needs to be invaded and transformed by the power of Christ and His Spirit. Again, as the old fisherman said, "make your call and election sure".

To me, Moses was a good example of a bold, courageous marketplace servant. Remember, a minister is one who serves God and His people. In contrast to what we discussed about ministers, I will touch on what it means to be a King (a marketplace servant) for the purpose of setting the foundation of this book. I will develop the role of a King later in the book.

A "King" is one who works fulltime in the marketplace. Kings may own or run companies, or work in maintenance. No matter the position or responsibility on the job, a King's role is to partner with the Pastor or Minister by reaching the lost and hurting people in the marketplace, developing disciples, holding Bible studies, praying, and helping to bring provision to the church to help further the Kingdom of God.

So you see why Moses is a great example of a "King". Moses is sent, not to Bible School or seminary, but to a monarch – Pharaoh (representing a world system) – with God's word in his mouth.

As we see in *Exodus 4:1-4*, Moses doubts his effectiveness as a leader, so God asks, *"What's in your hand?"* Moses replies *"A rod."* God is about to show Moses it's not just a piece of carved, dead wood. By God's power, it can be transformed into something alive and powerful - a serpent! What seemed mundane in Moses' hand became a mighty tool with God's touch.

Likewise, we all know the story of David and Goliath. David had a slingshot in his hand that proved very effective against God's enemy. Elisha carried the mantle of his former boss Elijah. Some of the disciples had fishermen's nets while others had a little boy's fishes and loaves. Paul was a tentmaker and, in one of my favorite stories from the Book of Judges, Samson used the jawbone of an ass.

What seems small in our hands – such as the widow's two mites – can be transformed into the "mighty" when given to God for the greater cause.

> "He who loves what he does never looks for work."
> - Confucius

CHAPTER 3
THE TURNING

The World: You are what you do.
The Gospel: Do what you are.
- Anonymous

GOT AN ITCH?

When you hear the name Michael Jordan, you immediately think basketball player. Not just any basketball player, but an extraordinarily gifted and successful superstar. In 1994, after ten years in the NBA, including a three-peat title run, Jordan tried to make it as a professional baseball player. It pained me to watch this amazing athlete, arguably the greatest basketball player of all time, swatting at a curve ball. He looked awkward, out of place, and definitely out of uniform. After a year of playing baseball, Michael returned to play basketball for a number of years, during which he led the Chicago Bulls to three additional championships.

Jerry Rice, with whom I've played a little golf, is the greatest wide receiver ever to play in the National Football League. Combined with his graceful, soft hands, he was always elusive after the catch. However, you may also recall that after his retirement from the NFL in 2006, Jerry attempted a run at becoming a professional golfer.

Jerry is a gifted athlete and a good golfer, but the gift for being a professional on the links wasn't there.

Now, I applaud the efforts of both Michael Jordan and Jerry Rice but the old saying comes to mind: If one gets an itch, scratch it, but don't scratch it until you bleed. We all have an area of strength — gifting if you will — and then we have hobbies and interests. The challenge for most of us is finding our strengths and gifts while making a good living - staying in our lane — versus just having a "job" and making a good living.

> "A career is something I choose for myself.
> A calling is something I receive.
> A career is something I do for myself.
> A calling is something I do for God.
> A calling lasts forever."
> - Anonymous

WHEN TO SWITCH GEARS

In 1966, I chose construction work. In 1977, I gave my life to the Lord. Shortly thereafter, I became filled with the Spirit. By 1978, God had called me to be a "Pastor" . . . (priest). You are probably asking yourself, "How did *that* happen?"

For thirty two years, I wondered and wandered. I was never quite sure where I fit in. In the 60's and early 70's, I lived a rather footloose and fancy-free life. Commitment and responsibility were not familiar ways to me then, at least not until I met and married my wife, Carla. She became the stabilizing factor in my life. I dabbled in the San Francisco Rock 'n Roll scene in the sixties and then attempted to ride rodeo bulls - eight seconds is an eternity on the back of a very agitated Brahma Bull! I even toyed with the idea of joining an infamous motorcycle club. Eventually, I decided to go back to school to learn about computer technology before changing my decision and working in construction from 1966-1980. Because I loved the outdoors and working with my hands, I began to realize that I'd landed my dream job as an ironworker. Although I never made a lot of money, I always had enough, and the thought of doing anything else never crossed my mind.

I have many fond memories of life in the mid-70's. We lived on Rosewood Lane in the small mountain hamlet called Paradise, California. My daughter, Sarah, was born there. A few days after her birth, while I was working 100 miles away in Sacramento, I received an emergency call from my sister-in-law saying that Carla had hemorrhaged, was in critical condition, and had been rushed to the hospital. I immediately ran out the door, jumped into my pickup truck and headed for the hospital. The drive seemed to take forever. In my frantic state I began talking to God and made a deal with Him that if He would heal my wife, I would do whatever He wanted.

I wasn't spiritual back then, but found myself desperately pleading with God for my wife. I certainly didn't give a second thought that

God would take me up on my offer. After all, *"What on earth could God do with me?"* I thought. *"Nothing! I'm not even in His league."*

Suddenly I became aware of my thoughts, and began to realize that I believed in the existence of God. Unbeknownst to me at the time, that was the beginning of my quest for God and His pursuit of me. You see, God healed my wife. He responded to my plea. As for me . . . well . . ..

For weeks I tried to get back into my normal routine. I went to work, spent time with family, and occasionally met the guys after work to blow off some steam. All the while, I kept thinking about God. *"Who is God anyway? Why is there a God? Where did He come from?"* I would catch myself staring at the sky wondering about this place called Heaven.

One clear Saturday in January, towards the end of duck season, as I sat in my blind watching the geese and duck migrate south, I thought to myself, *"Why do they do that? Is there really a God who controls nature?"* As my thoughts often turned toward questions about God, I began wondering where I fit in.

My wife began gently prodding me and, in 1977, I eventually gave in to the idea of going to church. From the day I was born again, I served the Lord by attending church, giving, volunteering with youth ministry, hosting weekly home Bible studies, and doing whatever else I could find time for. That same year, I was attending a church conference in Anaheim when God healed me of an irregular heartbeat. Everything in my life was changing, and I found myself feeling happy. Very happy!

One day while on a job in Calistoga, I began noticing that one by one, my longtime friends were taking pot shots at my new-found faith. *"Why all the antagonism?"* I wondered. Hugely disappointed, I tried being a sport about it, but realized it really hurt. As I drove back across the valley that evening toward Paradise, I came to this conclusion: my life had changed and would never be the same.

There were clues from God: I was saved, God healed me, and I was filled with the Holy Spirit. I had daily prayer time and listened to a lot of sermons on tape as well as worship music or my favorite contemporary Christian artist. I was a "Christian". I actually felt fulfilled; even content. But, what did it all mean?

A NEW DIRECTION

I'm sure Moses, after forty years out in the desert, felt somewhat the same until he witnessed the burning bush. My "burning bush" was a visitation from the Holy Spirit while driving in my old Nissan pickup truck at 5:30 one morning. I was heading towards Sacramento to retrofit the Capitol Rotunda after the big 7.0 Oroville earthquake when, all of a sudden, the inside of my truck lit up like a great light bulb. A "voice" - a presence - told me in plain language, *"Quit your job. Prepare yourself, for I have called you."* To this day, I am not sure exactly what happened. I'm still not sure if it was an angel or Christ himself. Whatever or whoever it was, it changed my life forever!

Even now, I am still surprised by my readiness and willingness to obey. I knew I wanted to keep the promise that I made to God the night He miraculously healed my wife but I had no idea what God's plans were for my life. In any case, for the first time in my life, with confidence that I still find hard to believe, I had a mission to the future.

I can recall telling my family, who were not saved at the time, that I was leaving my secure union job to move to Oklahoma to attend Bible School. It was 1978 and I had no promise of the future, yet I knew I was supposed to go and that God was calling me into full-time, pastoral ministry. There is a confidence in knowing, and you must have that knowledge before making a huge, life-changing decision.

Of all the things in the world, and of all people, God called me to preach and teach. Me - Dick Bernal - the person who is afraid of public speaking, microphones, and people staring at him. My familiar circles were the construction workers, bikers, country & western joints, and the rough and tumble, good ol' boys who were not known for oratory skills. I had given one speech in my life and it was a disaster. Sure, I could tell a joke or hold a conversation amongst friends, but teach or preach the Bible to others in front of a crowd? Unlike Moses, I didn't have an Aaron to whom I could pass the buck. What I did have was my faith in the God who saved me and a promise from His word:

> Then the word of the Lord came to me,
> saying: "Before I formed you in the womb I
> knew you; Before you were born I sanctified you;
> I ordained you a prophet to the nations." Then said I:
> "Ah, Lord God! Behold, I cannot speak, for I am a
> youth." But the Lord said to me: "Do not say, 'I am
> a youth,' For you shall go to all to whom I send you,
> And whatever I command you, you shall speak. Do
> not be afraid of their faces, For I am with you to
> deliver you," says the Lord. Then the Lord put forth
> His hand and touched my mouth, and the Lord said
> to me: "Behold, I have put My words in your mouth.
> See, I have this day set you over the nations and over
> the kingdoms, To root out and to pull down, To
> destroy and to throw down, To build and to plant."
> - Jeremiah 1:4-10

Looking back over the last thirty-plus years, I am still shocked at God's amazing grace in my life. It's as if God enjoys picking the least likely candidate to put in "office".

My construction career began when I attended Trade School in my mid-twenties. Two nights each week I attended a local community college for the "trades" while getting on-the-job experience working as an Apprentice. Back then I had a lot of energy, but by this time I was thirty-five, married with a wife and young child, and God was calling me to go back to school! Carla and I sat through two years of five hours a day, five days a week Bible School training.

For we are His workmanship, created in Christ Jesus
for good works, which God prepared beforehand
that we should walk in them.
- Ephesians 2:10

To my surprise, there were men, women, and couples much older than Carla and me at Bible School. Some had retired from their careers and wanted more Bible knowledge while others were simply bored with idleness and needed a jump start. Many of the younger students were not sure what they really wanted to do in life, but felt pressured to attend Bible school because they were PK's - preacher's kids. Many students quit school by Christmas break because they felt frustrated and thought they were wasting their time. I recall counseling one young fella who was battling whether or not to stay. His parents convinced him he was going to be a pastor but he wasn't "feeling it". I asked him what he did feel. He wasn't exactly sure in what capacity, but he loved business! I encouraged him to pursue his dream but he was completely stressed about disappointing his parents.

"If you don't know where you're
going, you will end up somewhere else."
- Yogi Berra

When school started again in January 1980, the young man didn't return to school. I've often wondered if he ever found his "sweet spot". My prayer is that this book will help others find theirs.

I didn't know my calling was going to bring me to Silicon Valley, deep in the heart of San Jose, California. I didn't know my calling was to pastor Jubilee Christian Center. But, I did know that I had to stay steadfast in order to reach my divine destination.

Perhaps you don't have a testimony yet. But you do have a calling. God has a plan for your future – whether King or Priest - that we can discover through His Word.

> "The question is not who you are going
> to be, but finding out who you already are."
> - Mike Fox

CHAPTER 4
BREAK ON THROUGH
TO THE OTHER SIDE

Then Elijah said to Ahab, "Go up, eat and drink;
for there is the sound of abundance of rain."
- 1 Kings 18:41

HUMBLE BEGINNINGS

There is a sound of abundance coming! Colonel Chuck Yeager broke the sound barrier in October 1947. Before then, many test pilots called the sound barrier the "demon wall" because so many of them died in fiery crashes trying to bust through it. However, once Colonel Yeager broke the barrier, an abundance of technological advances soon followed. Twenty-two short years later, Neal Armstrong walked on the moon, and today we are searching the far reaches of the universe.

Elijah broke through drought with a prophetic declaration, *"There is a sound of coming rain . . . in abundance!"* Funny that even after he said it the sky was still blue and cloudless. Several times Elijah told his servant to go back and look out across the Mediterranean Sea and each time the servant reported back that there was no change, no clouds. Finally, after seven times, a little cloud the size of a man's hand appeared. That was all the old prophet needed to hear.

His declaration wasn't that there was a small cloud somewhere off in the distance, rather, that there was the sound of *abundance of rain.*

Even great rivers have humble beginnings, but once they get rolling, the momentum is fierce. We call a river's flow its current. Isn't it interesting that money is referred to as currency? By design it's supposed to be constantly flowing, moving, and growing. God told Adam one of the rivers coming out of the Garden of Eden would lead to gold and precious gems.

> "The name of the first is Pishon; it is the one
> which skirts the whole land of Havilah, where
> there is gold. And the gold of that land is good.
> Bdellium and the onyx stone are there."
> - Genesis 2:11-12

The Hebrew word for "river" is *nahar,* which literally means *to sparkle, make cheerful, or prosperous.*

> "Blessed is the man Who walks not in the counsel
> of the ungodly, Nor stands in the path of sinners,
> Nor sits in the seat of the scornful; But his
> delight is in the law of the Lord, And in His law
> he meditates day and night. He shall be like a
> tree Planted by the rivers of water, That brings
> forth its fruit in its season, Whose leaf also shall
> not wither; And whatever he does shall prosper."
> - Psalm 1:1-3

The word for the tributary Pishon, means *to disperse or distribute*. In the garden, Adam and Eve had their needs met but if they wanted gold or precious stones, they had to follow the river Pishon. God gives opportunities with revelation. Prosperity is not a given or automatic simply because one is "saved, filled, and loves God." Everyone still has to go, search, dig, and keep digging. As vital and essential as faith, hope, and love are, we still need wisdom, knowledge, and understanding. Even in Paradise, the Garden of Eden, Adam had a job – tiller of the soil.

Rivers are like people. Some fast, some slow, some wide, some narrow, some deep, some shallow, some noisy, some quiet, some clear, some muddy. But all are water, and all rivers serve a purpose.

> "How precious is Your lovingkindness, O God!
> Therefore the children of men put their trust under
> the shadow of Your wings. They are abundantly
> satisfied with the fullness of Your house, And You
> give them drink from the river of Your pleasures."
> - Psalm 36:7-8

Right now, you might be dry and in a creative drought. Let me say this over you: I hear a sound of abundance coming. It may start off as a sprinkle, then a little creek, but it won't be long. You will be swept up in its glory.

> "He said to me, "Son of man, have you seen this?"
> Then he brought me and returned me to the bank of
> the river. When I returned, there, along the bank of
> the river, were very many trees on one side and the

other. Then he said to me: "This water flows toward the eastern region, goes down into the valley, and enters the sea. When it reaches the sea, its waters are healed. And it shall be that every living thing that moves, wherever the rivers go, will live. There will be a very great multitude of fish, because these waters go there; for they will be healed, and everything will live wherever the river goes. Along the bank of the river, on this side and that, will grow all kinds of trees used for food; their leaves will not wither, and their fruit will not fail. They will bear fruit every month, because their water flows from the sanctuary. Their fruit will be for food, and their leaves for medicine."
- Ezekiel 47:6-9, 12

"There's one thing stronger than all the armies of the world, and that's an idea whose time has come."
- Victor Hugo

CHAPTER 5
STAY IN YOUR LANE

"Philip found Nathanael and said to him, "We have found Him of whom Moses in the law, and also the prophets, wrote—Jesus of Nazareth, the son of Joseph." And Nathanael said to him, "Can anything good come out of Nazareth?" Philip said to him, "Come and see." Jesus saw Nathanael coming toward Him, and said of him, "Behold, an Israelite indeed, in whom is no deceit!" Nathanael said to Him, "How do You know me?" Jesus answered and said to him, "Before Philip called you, when you were under the fig tree, I saw you." Nathanael answered and said to Him, "Rabbi, You are the Son of God! You are the King of Israel!" Jesus answered and said to him, "Because I said to you, 'I saw you under the fig tree,' do you believe? You will see greater things than these." And He said to him, "Most assuredly, I say to you, hereafter you shall see heaven open, and the angels of God ascending and descending upon the Son of Man."
- John 1:45-51

ACHIEVING OPEN HEAVENS

Several years back, I wrote a book entitled, "Living Under An Open Heaven." Malachi promised such a blessing for tithers that we would be overwhelmed because of the open windows of heaven. Mark wrote of God's voice being heard and a dove descending on the recently baptized Jesus via an open heaven. John, in Revelation, looked and a door was open in heaven with Jesus beckoning him to *"come up here"* and see the future.

In the 28th chapter of Deuteronomy, God lays down the law of blessings and curses. The first fourteen verses are all good . . . if His people obeyed. However from verses 15 to 68, God sternly warns them about the consequences of disobedience.

I want to look with you at *Deuteronomy 28:23-24* where God is talking about a closed heaven. Why were the heavens closed? Sin and disobedience shut off our supply route from heaven to earth. He calls it a bronze heaven and iron earth! Brass, at times, represents sin, (i.e., brazen altar, brazen serpent). With no rain, or a closed heaven, the earth becomes parched and hard.

Now, back to Jesus's statement in *John 1:51* to a doubting Nathaniel, *"You shall see heaven open, and angels ascending and descending upon the Son of Man."* Jacob was the first to tell us about the trafficking of angels. He saw a ladder from earth to heaven with angelic beings traveling up and down. Jesus came to Israel in very tough times when the nation was under Roman rule of the wicked King Herod and surrounded by stiff-necked Pharisees. Despite all the sin around Him, Jesus didn't slow down one bit. Heaven stayed open and He lived and ministered under an open heaven. You and I can, too.

I live and pastor in Silicon Valley, in the shadow of San Francisco. Toto, this isn't Kansas! Bible Belt? We're not even the cuff on the trousers the belt holds up! Nevertheless, I've been teaching people how to keep heaven open in spite of all that's opposing God and His Kingdom.

Jesus walked fully in His calling and prophetic purpose. That, to me, is what keeps heaven open. If you're a priest, walk in your calling to the max. If you're a King, go for it with all the passion and energy God gives you. God has never given me a vision I could afford. I need provision. God's Kings bring in the spoils of victory from dominating the marketplace. When Kings and Priests cooperated through divine synergy in the Old Testament, Israel prospered tremendously. When roles were violated, Israel suffered.

> "Then David consulted with the captains of
> thousands and hundreds, and with every leader.
> And David said to all the assembly of Israel, "If it
> seems good to you, and if it is of the Lord our God,
> let us send out to our brethren everywhere who are
> left in all the land of Israel, and with them to the
> priests and Levites who are in their cities and their
> common-lands, that they may gather together to us;
> and let us bring the ark of our God back to us, for we
> have not inquired at it since the days of Saul." Then
> all the assembly said that they would do so, for the
> thing was right in the eyes of all the people."
> – 1 Chronicles 13:1-4

So far, so good. What a great idea. Let's all bring the ark home. Wow. Of course God would be pleased with this mission. Read on!

"So they carried the ark of God on a new cart from
the house of Abinadab, and Uzza and Ahio drove the
cart. 8 Then David and all Israel played music before
God with all their might, with singing, on harps, on
stringed instruments, on tambourines, on cymbals,
and with trumpets. 9 And when they came to
Chidon's[a] threshing floor, Uzza put out his hand
to hold the ark, for the oxen stumbled. 10 Then
the anger of the Lord was aroused against Uzza,
and He struck him because he put his hand to the
ark; and he died there before God. 11 And David
became angry because of the Lord's outbreak
against Uzza; therefore that place is called
Perez Uzza[b] to this day."
- I Chronicles 13:7-11

Hey, God, what's going on here? We thought you would like us to

have the ark back and in its proper place! David is angry at God so

he parks the ark!

"David was afraid of God that day, saying, "How
can I bring the ark of God to me?" So David would
not move the ark with him into the City of David,
but took it aside into the house of Obed-Edom the
Gittite. The ark of God remained with the family
of Obed-Edom in his house three months. And
the Lord blessed the house of Obed-Edom and
all that he had."
- 1 Chronicles 13:12-14

Ol' Obed-Edom hit the lottery! Three months of God's favor and

blessing. But David eventually read the Bible and three months later

he "gets it".

"David built houses for himself in the City of David;
and he prepared a place for the ark of God, and
pitched a tent for it. 2 Then David said, "No one
may carry the ark of God but the Levites, for the
Lord has chosen them to carry the ark of God and
to minister before Him forever." 3 And David
gathered all Israel together at Jerusalem, to
bring up the ark of the Lord to its place, which
he had prepared for it. 4 Then David assembled
the children of Aaron and the Levites."
- I Chronicles 15:1-4

Even though he is the King, David realizes the priests must carry the ark, not just any old Uzza. It was God's order of things. A major problem I see in America is the church has gone corporate. Well-meaning businessmen, "Kings," trying to do the work, or tell the pastors how to run the house of God.

IDENTIFYING YOUR LANE

Years ago I had a young pastor come to me for counseling, asking what he should do because his church board forbade him to mention Satan, demons, abortion, or homosexuality from the pulpit. I told him to resign and obey God by pioneering a church that was Bible-based and not corporately run! He did. I drove by his old church recently and saw it was closed. This is not an isolated incident in America.

Similar situations have happened to me from time to time. I had a member who insisted on seeing me once a month and who always came in with his laundry list of what was wrong with Jubilee. The music was too loud, the sermons too long, or this or that. For a while I listened and put up with his diatribe but finally I had enough and asked him how many churches he had pastored! None, of course. At that time, we were the fastest growing church in the Valley. Even our local newspaper, the *San Jose Mercury-News*, said we were the largest in the Valley and no church had ever grown as fast as Jubilee. To God be all the glory for sure!

I finally wised up and turned the tables on the guy by asking him what he would think about me visiting his company and telling him everything I thought he was doing wrong. I told him I figured he would laugh me out of his office because I knew nothing about his industry or how things worked at his company, but that I should trust that he did. When I asked him to trust me and trust that God was blessing our mission and vision, he left angry and I've not seen him since. I heard he tried to straighten out a couple of other local churches, but after they gave him the left foot of fellowship, he moved out of the area.

Being successful in business does not carry over into church growth success. As a swimmer and water polo player back in high school, I was assigned a lane to swim in during meets. If, for some reason, we intruded into someone else's lane, we would be automatically disqualified. Longtime friend Steve Hage, Pastor of Jubilee Orange County, puts it this way, *"Man, just stay in your lane."* Let's appreciate each other's gifting and anointing. Here's a list that helps me:

PRIEST	KING
Carried the responsibilities of hearing from God for the people.	Destroyed the enemies of God.
Offered sacrifices to God for the people.	Brought the spoils of war to the House of God.
Told the people what the Lord was saying.	Governed the physical affairs of the nation.
Received tithes and offerings from the people.	Protected the people and the priest.
Took care of the House of God.	Brought tithes and offerings to the House of God.
Spoke encouragement to the Kings and warriors before or during battle.	

CHAPTER 6
CULTURE SHIFT

Arise, shine; For your light has come!
And the glory of the Lord is risen upon you.
For behold, the darkness shall cover the earth,
And deep darkness the people;
- Isaiah 60:1

Notice that first the church "rises" before the shining comes. Faith acts . . . stands . . . rises . . . then moves!

It's our turn! Time for the church to rise up, the devil to shut up, and demons to sit down and keep quiet. Everyone is attracted to bright things. A burning bush caught Moses's attention. The wise Kings of the east followed a bright star. The Church was birthed with a sound and quite a sight with tongues of fire. Here, we see in the last days the bright burning church attracts kings as well as lost or backslidden family members.

Who, here in America, doesn't love the 4th of July and its fireworks? It's a big holiday for my family, especially the grandkids. We make sure the barbecue and watermelon are all finished by dark with no interruptions! Then, it's show time!

A COUNTER-CULTURE

A church is truly a Kingdom City set on a hill, beckoning one and all to come! But church is much more than two hours on Sunday morning. Gatherings are good and healthy. We were built for community and cross-pollination, but let's not think a visit to a building with a cross on it satisfies our Creator.

Some have erroneously gone too far with this and have declared church, as we have known it, passé. Nothing could be further from the truth. A fella once wanted to debate me by using the worn-out cliché of not believing in organized religion. Knowing he didn't have a clue what he was talking about, I asked him what he had against "organization" – the opposite being chaos, of course. I pressed further, asking if he would tolerate disorganized government, schools, traffic, air control, or perhaps his own business. He quickly changed the course of the conversation by adding that what he really meant was he didn't want some church trying to control him and tell him how to live his life. Me neither! I sure don't want some man, woman, or organization to control me either, but I do need help from God and so does everyone else. By the end of our discussion, he actually admitted he might pop in to Jubilee for a look-see. I told him of course I'd be honored to host him, but chided him by adding that he should be careful because he might just like it!

On another occasion, one young zealot tried to convince me that God was through with church buildings and church gatherings. He had a small house prayer group of like-minded idealists who felt superior in their "revelation" about what God was really doing. It's a form of Kingdom anarchy. I've been around a long time and there's nothing new under the sun. My response was simply to tell him I didn't think he got out much. One of my pastor friends said, "Wait until he grows up, gets married, and has a real job, kids, and responsibilities! Welcome to Planet Earth! He will probably attend a church his family wants to go to and hopefully will retain passion and fire for prayer and revival."

There will always be Sunday morning worship services all around the world. Even if church attendance is dwindling in America, it's not worldwide. Churches that are relevant, on fire, and changing lives are growing and are historical. Jesus told us to "go" into all the world and make disciples. He didn't say go to work, have fun on Saturdays, and go to church on Sunday morning. Although none of that is bad or wrong, what's vitally important is how we share our faith Monday to Sunday.

Whether you're a King-Priest or Priest-King like me, we all have the ministry of reconciliation and are charged to engage culture - not as a sub-culture, but as a counter-culture. I would like to add that it's an "attractive" counter-culture with an attractive message.

TIME TO SHIFT

I came to Christ and His church in 1977, broken and fragmented. Looking back on my life, having a good time came naturally. Having way too much of a good time became habitual. I needed to be "discipled." I thank God for my early church families. Three and a half years after salvation and infilling of the spirit, I was pastoring a small flock of family and friends. I had to be healed so I could be a healer. Our church's unspectacular origin mirrored a phenomenon about to burst upon the world. Silicon Valley! When I grew up here, it was called the "Valley of Heart's Delight". Fruit orchards dominated the landscape for decades. Since the turn of the last century, San Francisco was "The City", 45 miles north, while San Jose and the smaller towns around were simply the window dressing to "Paris of the West".

It wasn't long after the silicon chip came along that we began to hear of new startups like Apple, Intel, and others that today dominate the market in their particular field. Our campus is a rock's throw from some of the most famous companies in the world. A new "culture" emerged right before our eyes as we struggled to birth a church and impart revelation that would change the world.

CHAPTER 7
LORD, HELP ME FIND MY SWEET SPOT
(A GOLFER'S PRAYER)

Conviction should always be at the heart of your
vocation, and the added benefit is that you will be
more productive in all of your endeavors.
- Anonymous

All of the following renowned Bible characters knew exactly who
they were in their callings. They weren't double-minded. They
didn't wonder, *"Gee, should I be doing this and not that; maybe I'm
not pleasing God."* Let's examine whether they were businessmen
(kings) or priests unto God.

> **Abraham**: A man of God who was a businessman. He was
> not a priest.

> **Melchizedek**: A priest. Uniquely, Melchizedek was also king
> of Salem, a king-priest. He's interesting because he was a
> type of Christ.

> **Isaac**: A businessman.

> **Jacob:** A businessman.

> **Joseph**: A businessman - superb one at that.

> **Moses**: A businessman. Although Moses shepherded the
> people of Israel, he was first a prince of Egypt. Afterwards,

for 40 years Moses was an "aggie". He raised sheep in the agriculture trade!

David: A man of God, but Israel's king.

Solomon: David's son, who was also a king.

Elisha: A businessman. Later, he was called out of farming to be God's prophet.

Peter and John: Businessmen, i.e. fishermen. Later, in due course, they were called out of the fishing industry into fulltime ministry.

Jesus: Called out of construction work (I can relate), then began His period of ministry.

KEEP YOUR DAY JOB (THE DOCTOR IS IN)

In 1996, Carla and I went to Pensacola, Florida to witness the great revival that broke out and continued there for several years.

One night, following the preaching, worship and prayer time, the pastor had us break up into groups of four or five people so that we could pray for each other. One dear lady in our group was sobbing uncontrollably. Carla tried to comfort her. I thought someone had died, or that she just learned that she had a terminal disease.

When she was finally able to compose herself she said: "My husband is suicidal, and he's a pastor! He was a very successful doctor, and he loved God. He witnessed to everybody that came to our office, prayed for people, and held Bible studies. There was this lady — I think she called herself a prophetess — she prophesied and said to my husband, "You are out of God's will. You are disobeying God. You're called to the ministry." So my husband quit his practice and started a church. Now, two years later, there are only fifty people attending the church. We're starving, behind on our bills, and he's suicidal because he wants so bad to obey God."

I asked for her name, and she said it was Georgia. "Georgia," I said, "Go back home and tell your husband to shut down that church. He's not a priest. He's out of order. He's doing something that he's not called to do. He was called to be a doctor."

The story of Georgia's husband is a good example of a marketplace king. Her husband was tithing to his local church, was getting more people saved and doing more for the Kingdom of God and his community as a doctor than as a so-called pastor. He was anointed to plant himself in the marketplace, not to be serving as a priest. Simply because this Christian doctor passionately loved God didn't necessarily mean that he should quit his job and start a church.

On another occasion, a dear friend of mine who attends Marilyn Hickey's church in Denver, Colorado told me about his business partner. My friend, David, shared that his partner would not attend church. Although he was raised in church, he just wouldn't attend. He told David, *"I know how it is. I'm going to go to church. I'm going to get the Holy Ghost. I'm going to go crazy, which means I'm going to have to quit my job and move to Africa to be a missionary."* David explained to him that he could be both – a good businessman, and a good Christian, but he wasn't convinced. In this man's mind serving the Lord meant having to be a preacher.

As it turns out, I was later invited to speak at a two-night conference at Marilyn's church and spoke on the topic of *"Kings and Priests."* David bought the tapes, gave them to his friend, and thankfully he listened. David shared with me that his friend was in church the very next Sunday with new-found freedom. This dear Christian man realized that he could fall in love with Jesus without any unintended consequences! He could indeed love doing what he was really called to be, a king, and thereby bring provision to support the vision of the House of God in his community.

What's important to you? Do you want to use the talents and natural gifts God gave you? If it's job satisfaction, then like these two professionals, bring God to the marketplace with you. There's never a reason to feel guilty or become double-minded about your calling, but you may need to keep your day job!

TRANSITIONING FROM KING TO PRIEST

Similarly, I have witnessed novel cases of change in one's vocation. There are some people in the marketplace who, in the fullness of time, recognize God's call to the pulpit. Jubilee's Pastor Randy Estrada is a good example. Randy began his career as a policeman in Oakland, California. He found complete fulfillment in his role. After serving for several years in our small group cell system, Randy and his wife, Mae, had several hundred people attending small groups under their leadership. I saw the potential in Randy's pastoral calling, and following several years of spiritual mentoring, Randy realized the calling to change vocations and serve as a priest unto God. Today, many years later, Randy still serves on our pastoral team.

Another staff pastor, Chris Cobb, used to work in Silicon Valley's high-tech industry making a great living. Today, he could still make great money, but Pastor Chris also realized his call to serve God in the ministry fulltime.

Don't overlook the fact that it is so much easier to do what you are "called" to do rather than trying to do something in another calling.

Let me go back to professional sports for another example. Charles Barkley is a basketball legend. But if you've ever seen Charles Barkley swing a golf club, he looks like an old lawn chair unfolding. On his downswing he looks like someone trying to swat mosquitoes! Now contrast that with Tiger Woods swinging a golf club. His swing is akin to poetry in motion.

When you perform what you are called to do, and in the area God has gifted you, beautiful rhythm is created and you appear so natural in your setting.

Saints, if you are called to business, then be first-rate at what you do. Do you drive a truck? Then be the best truck driver you can, and be a good witness for the Lord up and down the highway. In fact, most goods and services within cities are delivered by truck! Are you called to be a carpenter's helper or called to the hospitality industry? Perhaps you are dreaming of running your own Starbucks franchise? You may naturally analyze or have an engineering mind and would love the opportunity to compete with Microsoft or IBM but on a much smaller scale. No matter your natural gifting and desire, God doesn't care if you make a million dollars; and, it doesn't bother God if you have an ingenious idea for thinner circuit boards, creative new apps, or cloud computing. Just remember, it was God who gifted you with that imagination.

The point is, the respective gifts, talents, and skills come with God's selection and calling of each and every person. You have them. Use them, and be liberated in your calling.

A UNIQUE HISTORIC TIDBIT

Sarah Edwards, wife of the famous 18th century preacher Jonathan Edwards had eleven children. From their offspring they produced:

> Scores of preachers, thirteen college presidents, sixty-five professors, one hundred lawyers, the dean of a law school, thirty judges, sixty-six physicians, the dean of a medical school, and eighty public office holders. But that's not all; there were three mayors, three governors, three United States senators, one comptroller of the United States Treasury, and one Vice President of the United States.

While the Edwards family produced many preachers, they also influenced their communities in the marketplace. Now, that's wonderful spiritual influence!

CHAPTER 8
MONEY: A TOOL AND A TOY

Beloved, I pray that you may prosper in all things
and be in health, just as your soul prospers.
- 3 John 2 (KJV)

THE RIGHT TOOLS OF A KING

John's friend Gaius was a wonderful Christian. The Gaius of Romans 16:23 is probably one in the same. As we read on in John's 3rd Epistle, vs. 5-8, Gaius was generous, loving, even to strangers, and a true leader. Gaius was more than likely a businessman (King) for John says, *"Beloved, I pray above all things that you prosper."* The Greek word here is *"to have a prosperous, fruitful journey (life) and succeed financially in your business affairs."*

It's one thing to be kind and caring, but without finances to share, it's merely a feeling. In an earlier chapter, I discussed the first of four rivers coming out of Eden mentioned in Genesis 2 — the "Pishon". *"Follow Pishon,"* God suggested, *"and you will find gold (good gold) as well as other valuable commodities."*

Do you know money is mentioned more times in the Bible than any other subject including faith, hope, healing, heaven, or hell? Why? I believe it is because money touches just about every area of our lives and it dictates the quality of life, to a large degree, here on earth. Solomon put it this way:

> For wisdom is a defense as money is a defense,
> But the excellence of knowledge is that wisdom
> gives life to those who have it.
> - Ecclesiastes 7:12.

> A feast is made for laughter, And wine makes
> merry; But money answers everything.
> - Ecclesiastes 10:19.

Jesus tells us "to make friends with unrighteous mammon." He also charges us to "give" to it can come back multi-fold. Money is a tool and a toy. It is to work for us and produce, but also it is for enjoyment and pleasure.

A local multimillionaire here in Silicon Valley gave me 5 million dollars from his personal wealth. I, in turn, gave it to my church. First, it's a tool. I needed to pay off a chunk of very expensive, prime real estate so we could build God's house.

But, it's also for pleasure. I love when I can take the family and grandkids on a nice vacation and still pay my tithes, give offerings, help the needy and save some!

God has never given me a "vision" I could afford. I needed to stretch my "faith" and believe God for provision for the vision! That's why I am constantly encouraging my "Kings" to believe for more finances in their businesses so they can give more to the work of the Lord.

In Dr. Cho's church on Yoida Island, Seoul, Korea, *3 John 1-2* is over the entrance to the Sanctuary. In the late 50's after the Korean War, Korea was the second poorest country in the world. Dr. Cho began preaching prosperity, healing, and Holy Spirit power to a handful of poor refugees. Some of those young, poor men went on to become multimillionaires and some even billionaires. His prophetic, visionary preaching lit a fire under many and they in turn financed one of the great church campuses in the world.

I see one of my "callings" is to push and lean on "Kings" to grow and dream, and produce for the glory of the Kingdom and Christ our King-Priest.

> "The tragedy of man is what dies
> inside himself while he still lives."
> - Albert Schweitzer

CHAPTER 9
ENGAGING CULTURES
AND ADDRESSING STRONGHOLDS

"And He said to them, "Go into all the world and
preach the gospel to every creature. He who
believes and is baptized will be saved; but he
who does not believe will be condemned."
- Mark 16:15-16

Here, in *Mark 16:15*, kosmos means *"world"*. In *Matthew 28:19*
Jesus charges us to make disciples of all nations. Ethnos means
"nations". Jesus is telling us to invade the world - its cultures,
societies, racial diversities, and religions - as salt and light. Go into
corruption and darkness. Every nation has sectors or social
groupings that make up society:

- Government
- Business (commerce)
- Religion(s)
- Media
- Sports
- Art & Entertainment
- Education

In *Acts 2:17*, God promises to visit all flesh with an outpouring of His
Spirit. Paul tells us in *Romans 2:4* that it's the goodness of God that
leads to change. To impact a culture with its strongholds and

traditions one must be sensitive and discerning to the region's lifestyle (Nation/City).

SHIFTING MINDSETS

Before I made my first trip to India in 1982, in order to know a little about these precious people I would soon fall in love with, I read books, ate Indian food, and learned something about Hinduism. I found out Indian people love stories so I laced my messages with stories of my life - some funny, some serious, some challenging - so I could find common ground and gain trust before I threw out the "net".

As of late, I have spent a great deal of time in Mexico and Central and South America. Again, I study the various cultures of the particular cities (and nations) in which I would be ministering before traveling to each location. I feel it's important to understand what the people's greatest needs are, their traditional religion, economic challenges, strongholds (alcohol, drugs, domestic violence), and so on. During every conference or crusade, I conduct a business meeting to gather the "Kings", just as I do on a regular basis with business movers and shakers from Silicon Valley.

Often when I travel, I will take business leaders from my church to give testimonies and hold classes to encourage the locals that they too have a ministry as vital and important as the pastor. One of the challenges I face in developing nations is how to help believers to be unafraid of the world we are called back to. Traditional religion teaches that once saved and sanctified, a person should stay away from sinners and the sinful world, yet come to church as much as possible and be inoculated from evil. The problem with this mentality is that it's totally opposite of what Jesus commanded. Unfortunately, it's the pastors who keep this mindset going for whatever reason, whether fear, insecurity, or ego - who knows? Hopefully, it's simply ignorance of scripture. Here's how I see believers becoming "attractive".

- Be holy, yet relevant.
- Be different, yet not weird.
- Love God, and the world He loves.
- Spend time at church, but also with family, church friends, and unsaved friends.
- Pray, worship, and have fun.
- Be devout, but not self-righteous.
- Have discernment, but don't be judgmental.

WORKING TOGETHER

Jesus had no problem engaging culture. Whether He was in the Galilee region with conniving people, or Jerusalem with the leaders of the Nation, Decapolis with the Hellenists, or Samaria with the undesirables, He didn't change. They did!

As agents (ambassadors) of change, we must be sure of our message and discerning in our methods. I'm a life-long fisherman.

At six years of age, I learned how to catch blue gill out of a lake near our house. I made my own hooks out of clothes pins, cut a willow branch from Grandma's backyard to make a pole, used a ping pong ball for a bobber, and dug my own worms. I would bring home six to twelve little blue gills and beg Grandma or Mom to fry 'em up!

Later, as I really got into it, I became a fairly skilled fisherman. I have fished the world, literally, and have even gotten my whole family involved. Even Carla and my daughter Sarah, to this day, love trout fishing in the Sierras. Fish, like people, are different. Some are timid. Others aggressive. They have very diverse eating habits. That's why in my tackle box I have an assortment of "bait". We call them "lures" because we want to lure the fish to strike (bite). Some fish prefer live bait. People behave similarly. They are as different as fish and, if you put the wrong bait in front of them, forget it! With the right bait (message) though, watch them bite! We Kings and Priests need to learn how to fish . . . together!

> "Then He said to them, "Follow Me,
> and I will make you fishers of men."
> - Matthew 4:19

CHAPTER 10
FINDING COMMON GROUND

You have a hole . . . we fill it.
(From a paving company slogan)

Recently, I was in Singapore with Dr. Yonggi Cho, Dr. Paul Kim and several friends attending a conference hosted by Kong Hee. One of the speakers was A.R. Bernard of New York, a very gifted pastor who has a track record of impacting his city, much like Kong, who has tremendously influenced Singapore, along with Joseph Prince and other great leaders. I was taking notes as fast as I could to add knowledge to what I have already experienced in Silicon Valley. One of the speakers put up a slide, with information I'd like to share with you. This is a comparison of things important to the church and the world:

CHURCH	WORLD
Holiness	Happiness
Doctrine	Philosophy
Presence (worship)	Feeling Good
The Anointing	Entertainment
Evangelism	Privacy
Discipleship	Education
Fellowship	Cliques
Giving	Making Money
Heaven	Earth
Saving Man	Everything but man

Faithfulness	Fun
Tradition	Exploration (the new)

How do we engage culture in a relevant manner without being weird, yet maintaining our values? We find middle ground in the following areas:

- Family
- Health & Fitness
- Finance/Money
- Friends
- Love of Sports
- Hobbies
- Entertainment (dining, movies, hanging out)
- Civic and World Events
- Vacations
- Education
- Politics
- Death

ARE YOU ATTRACTIVE?

Sixty percent of the world is under the age of twenty-six. Eighty percent of new converts worldwide are fourteen and younger. To attract the young, we must find "felt needs" and speak a language they understand. A story I've heard over and over again from parents is that they raised their kids in church, but once they reached the ages of fourteen to nineteen, the young adults wanted nothing to do with church. However, the kids maintained their belief in God.

This scenario is played out across America and is very obvious in Europe. There are, in my opinion, several reasons why this happens. Churches ignore the young and their needs because of a lack of money, vision, or because of ignorance. When money is tight, the first things to go are usually the budgets for children and youth.

A friend of many years, Pastor Steve Hage, had a youth ministry with more kids involved and attending church than the senior pastor had adults. Because of the senior pastor's intimidation by Steve's success, he unceremoniously fired Steve, which ultimately led to the disbandment of the youth ministry.

Danny Silk from Bethel in Redding said, "We aren't just raising kids. We're raising future parents and grandparents." If you don't see the value of the emerging generation of "Kings and Priests", we will lose an army of Christian soldiers who should build on the foundation we laid.

Recently, I was driving down from Sacramento to San Jose on Highway 99. I noticed an abandoned construction project site. The foundation and parking lot were built but the steel beams had been left stacked up and were rusted out. After asking a friend what happened, I learned that the site was intended to be a large shopping mall, but the company had run out of funding. During my trips abroad, I noticed old, historical, beautiful church buildings that had long ceased holding services and had been converted to theaters, restaurants, and even mosques. Chills ran down my spine as I thought, *"Dear God, may this never happen in America."*

The famous actress of yesteryear, Mae West, said, "I used to be Snow White, but I drifted." Some people today are saying, "The church used to be relevant, but now . . . "

CHAPTER 11
IN HIS IMAGE, WE HAVE IMAGINATION

Truly God is good to Israel, To such as are
pure in heart. But as for me, my feet had
almost stumbled; My steps had nearly slipped
For I was envious of the boastful, When I saw
the prosperity of the wicked. For there are no
pangs in their death, But their strength is firm.
They are not in trouble as other men, Nor are
they plagued like other men. Therefore pride
serves as their necklace; Violence covers them
like a garment. Their eyes bulge with abundance;
They have more than heart could wish. They
scoff and speak wickedly concerning oppression;
They speak loftily. They set their mouth against
the heavens, And their tongue walks through the
earth. Therefore his people return here, and
waters of a full cup are drained by them. And
they say, "How does God know? And is there
knowledge in the Most High?" Behold, these
are the ungodly, Who are always at ease;
They increase in riches.
- Psalm 73:1-12

NOT JUST SAVED . . . CALLED

Have you ever, like Asaph here in Psalm 73, wondered about the
prosperity and success of people who don't know God? They're
secular "Kings" - powerful, famous, influential movers and shakers
of nations throughout the world. Granted, some are nicer than
others; maybe they're even generous to certain popular causes

such as eco-system, hunger, disease, etc., but they are not believers. God gets no credit or glory for their immense success. It's easy to write them off as "full of the devil" but let's not take the easy out just yet. A closer look at Cain in *Genesis 4:6-14* might help us to understand just how much of God is still in fallen man!

> "So the Lord said to Cain, "Why are you angry? And why has your countenance fallen? If you do well, will you not be accepted? And if you do not do well, sin lies at the door. And its desire is for you, but you should rule over it." Now Cain talked with Abel his brother;[a] and it came to pass, when they were in the field, that Cain rose up against Abel his brother and killed him. Then the Lord said to Cain, "Where is Abel your brother?" He said, "I do not know. Am I my brother's keeper?" And He said, "What have you done? The voice of your brother's blood cries out to Me from the ground. So now you are cursed from the earth, which has opened its mouth to receive your brother's blood from your hand. When you till the ground, it shall no longer yield its strength to you. A fugitive and a vagabond you shall be on the earth." And Cain said to the Lord, "My punishment is greater than I can bear! Surely You have driven me out this day from the face of the ground; I shall be hidden from Your face; I shall be a fugitive and a vagabond on the earth, and it will happen that anyone who finds me will kill me."
> - Genesis 4:6-14

Does Cain become a homeless, begging drunk or addict? Not according to *Genesis 4:16-17*.

"Then Cain went out from the presence of the Lord
and dwelt in the land of Nod on the east of Eden.
And Cain knew his wife, and she conceived and bore
Enoch. And he built a city, and called the name of the
city after the name of his son — Enoch."
- Genesis 4:16-17

Cain starts a family and is the first city builder in history. God's creative ability is still in him. Every human is created in the image and likeness of God to some degree. Now, because of sin and its power, we have babies born with challenges and traits that may be abnormal, but everything that lives still has God's fingerprints on it. Look at Cain's descendants in *Genesis 4:17-22*.

"And Cain knew his wife, and she conceived and bore
Enoch. And he built a city, and called the name of
the city after the name of his son—Enoch. To Enoch
was born Irad; and Irad begot Mehujael, and
Mehujael begot Methushael, and Methushael begot
Lamech. Then Lamech took for himself two wives:
the name of one was Adah, and the name of the
second was Zillah. And Adah bore Jabal. He was the
father of those who dwell in tents and have livestock.
His brother's name was Jubal. He was the father of
all those who play the harp and flute. And as for
Zillah, she also bore Tubal-Cain, an instructor of
every craftsman in bronze and iron. And the sister
of Tubal-Cain was Naamah."
- Genesis 4:17-22

We see the advent of commerce, employment, arts, and crafts. In Genesis 10, we are introduced to one of God's heroes, Noah. One chapter later we meet Nimrod, the first "leader" who begins to create a "worldly culture" or secondary culture to God's plan of a "Kingdom Culture". Even though man is fallen, he is still brilliant. In man is the urge to create, invent, produce, and build. Some do it better than others, but it's in all mankind. God's original plan for man to subdue and have dominion has been misdirected by dictators or depots since the time of Nimrod to this very day. Others who have no other agenda than to be successful have simply tapped into the creativity of God, but think it's all their own ability.

Why aren't more movers and shakers from the seven main sectors of society attracted to church? Here's my take: the world is attracted to beauty, order, intellect, professionalism, art, motivation, inventiveness, energy, and fun – not old, stale, religion with worn out do's and don'ts!

One pastor wrote, "The world would still rather buy a ticket for the Titanic than Noah's Ark." To try to scare the world into our rubber raft churches with our 'hang on until Jesus comes' mentality is not working.

Most of us have heard of the term Spirit-filled. That's what we label a church or ministry that is Pentecostal, neo-Pentecostal, or Charismatic in expression and that believes in the gifts of the spirit, invites presence, and divine power into their brand of church. These type churches point to Acts 2 as the headwaters of their beliefs.

> "When the Day of Pentecost had fully come, they
> were all with one accord in one place. And suddenly

there came a sound from heaven, as of a rushing
mighty wind, and it filled the whole house where
they were sitting. Then there appeared to them
divided tongues, as of fire, and one sat upon each
of them. And they were all filled with the Holy
Spirit and began to speak with other tongues, as
the Spirit gave them utterance."
- Acts 2:1-4

This is the genesis of the New Testament church - a rather spectacular kick-off to say the least. Obedience to the Lord (Acts 1:4-5), prayer, patience, the appointed day (the Day of Pentecost had fully come), and then suddenly a sound, a sight, a filling, and an outpouring throughout the city.

Notice, the house was filled before the people were (Acts 1:2). Here, I see a principle which is found in other places in the Bible. In *I Kings 8:1-13*, the Ark, representing God's presence, is brought to the Temple and put in its proper place (I Kings 8:6). Notice, after all this, the cloud filled the house of the Lord to a point where the priests could not function traditionally. That's what happens when we allow God to fill our churches with the cloud of His presence - tradition and routine take a back seat. I will admit this can be a little unnerving to a senior pastor who likes order.

ARISE!

I'll never forget the night we had a well-known guest minister from Tulsa, Oklahoma in service and I was very excited to hear him preach. I noticed the worship was much more intense than usual. People came to service ready to receive, with anticipation that filled the atmosphere. I found myself face down on the floor unable to move. My mind was telling me to get up and handle service and I questioned what my guest might be thinking. Yet, I couldn't budge. Then, I began to giggle like a school girl. I thought for sure my guest must think I'm nuts and that our church is one of those crazymatic ones, but there was nothing I could do but lay there and laugh. When I finally somewhat gained my composure and looked around, I noticed our guest slumped over in his chair laughing like he had just heard the funniest joke ever told. I don't recall if he ever did preach that night, but I do remember it was one powerful night.

> Until now you have asked nothing in My name.
> Ask, and you will receive, that your joy may be full."
> - John 16:24

Another place in the Bible that illustrates the law of filling is in *John 2*, the wedding in Cana, our Lord's first recorded miracle.

> "On the third day there was a wedding in Cana of
> Galilee, and the mother of Jesus was there. Now
> both Jesus and His disciples were invited to the
> wedding. And when they ran out of wine, the mother
> of Jesus said to Him, "They have no wine." Jesus said
> to her, "Woman, what does your concern have to do
> with Me? My hour has not yet come." His mother
> said to the servants, "Whatever He says to you, do
> it." Now there were set there six waterpots of stone,

according to the manner of purification of the Jews,
containing twenty or thirty gallons apiece. Jesus said
to them, "Fill the waterpots with water." And they
filled them up to the brim."
- John 2:1-7

What caught my attention in this famous account is that the water didn't turn into wine until there was a "filling" to the brim. No cup runneth over without first a filling. Whether you are a King-Priest or a Priest-King, we all need to be filled.

One night, Carla and I were having dinner in Napa Valley with Bill and Beni Johnson from Bethel Church in Redding, California. We were discussing this over a fine meal when Bill asked, "Dick, have you ever noticed the first spirit-filling recorded in the Bible was the Artisan commissioned to help build the Tabernacle with Moses?" I had to admit that I'd never noticed. Let's take a look at *Exodus 28:3*, followed by *Exodus 35:31-35*.

"So you shall speak to all who are gifted artisans,
whom I have filled with the spirit of wisdom, that
they may make Aaron's garments, to consecrate
him, that he may minister to Me as priest."
- Exodus 28:3

"...and He has filled him with the Spirit of God, in
wisdom and understanding, in knowledge and all
manner of workmanship, to design artistic works,
to work in gold and silver and bronze, in cutting
jewels for setting, in carving wood, and to work in
all manner of artistic workmanship. "And He has

79

> put in his heart the ability to teach, in him and
> Aholiab the son of Ahisamach, of the tribe of Dan.
> He has filled them with skill to do all manner of
> work of the engraver and the designer and the
> tapestry maker, in blue, purple, and scarlet thread,
> and fine linen, and of the weaver—those who do
> every work and those who design artistic works."
> - Exodus 35:31-35

These artists and craftsmen were "filled" to help build the house of the Lord (Tabernacle). Why is it that some of today's most gifted artisans stay far away from God's people and God's house? The world celebrates beauty and creativity whereas the traditional church has settled for the drab and mundane all in the name of holiness and humility. The church has lost her shine! One of my personal favorite passages in the Old Testament is *Isaiah 60:1-2*. Notice, there must be an "arising" before the "shining". Our part is to arise. God's part is to bring the shine.

CHAPTER 12
WOW! NOW I SEE!

"After these things I looked, and behold, a door
standing open in heaven. And the first voice
which I heard was like a trumpet speaking with
me, saying, "Come up here, and I will show
you things which must take place after this."
- Revelation 4:1

Jesus wanted John to see the future because revelation brings elevation. *"Come up here. I want to be up there."* John first saw an open door. I believe God has doors for all of us that He will open so we can have influence in our region and beyond. We are agents of change. Christianity is to be offered, not forced; demonstrated, not dictated; embraced and not manipulated. It's about self-denial, not self-fulfillment; sacrifice, not just success.

THE PURPOSE OF INFLUENCE

Franklin Faler once said, *"Kindness has converted more sinners than zeal, eloquence, or education."* I was speaking in Bogota, Colombia years ago, along with a number of leaders from all over the world. Pastor John Hagee and I were having fellowship after one of the sessions when he asked me this question, *"How do you turn church members into Christians?"* All I could do was stare at him! Then we both had a good belly laugh. Good question!

Church members are interested in their church, their personal growth, family needs, and they hope for the best. All of that is good, but Christians should also be aggressive in social revolution and cultural transformation. To engage society and impact culture as well as confront spiritual strongholds, we all must be ready to leave our comfort zone. For whatever reason, I've been given open doors into a wide variety of worlds - from politics, sports, entertainment, business, media, and even to the biker culture. Friendship evangelism has always worked best for me. I've heard Bill Hybels, Casey Treat, Kong Hee, and even the great Billy Graham, talk about finding common ground with people from every slice of life to create an open door for the Gospel of Christ.

Throughout the years I've been privileged to host President Bill Clinton for a fundraiser at Jubilee. I've hunted with Supreme Court Justice Antonin Scalia, golfed with Jim Brown, Smokey Robinson, and Bill Russell, worked closely with M.C. Hammer at Jubilee, dined with the Samsung family, Katy Perry and her parents, and recently welcomed more than 3,000 Hells Angels to my church as we buried an old friend. I am comfortable with the great, the famous, the talented, the powerful, and the rich just as much as I am with a homeless person. Jesus loves them all and we are all called to be ready to have a word, a prayer, a handshake, a hug, or even just a smile to show that the Jesus who lives in us also died for them!

CONCLUSION

"Therefore, if anyone is in Christ, he is a new
creation; old things have passed away; behold,
all things have become new."
- 2 Corinthians 5:17

Christ is in the business of giving new true identities. I saw a bumper sticker on a pastor's wife's car once that said, "Shift Happens". I thought it was because she drove a sporty little car with a stick shift. Carla cracked up and explained to me that it was actually part of their church slogan, "Shift and Change!" Their ministry was helping old, traditional churches and leaders branch out to develop new cultures. Culture shift! Nobody fights change more than church people. I will say it again, NOBODY! Ha!

Through the years of pastoring, mentoring, and teaching around the world, I've observed many churches and leaders who needed to grow, needed resources, volunteers, and the vibrant presence of God. But very few were willing to change and pay the price of "shifting" because they realized the shift would definitely upset the rank and file and defy tradition.

Previously I mentioned that I've loved the outdoors since childhood. For years I have enjoyed fishing, hunting, hiking, and golfing. In my early forties, several friends tried to get me to take up snow skiing. Several questions crossed my mind: *"Have you seen those wipeouts on television? Who has time to take on a new challenge? Do I really want to drive in all that snow? What if I break an arm or leg, or worse?"* My mind was made up. I would hate skiing. But my friends were relentless! After constant badgering, I caved in. That was more than twenty years ago and, guess what? I absolutely loved it — so much so that I got my entire family involved and now my grandkids want to learn!

As we age, we like what's familiar. Our tendencies are to stick with what we know, and what makes us feel safe. It's our comfort zone.

When is the last time you did something for the first time with God or for God? Recently, I heard a pastor say, *"A poverty spirit is more than a fear of lack of money. It's a lack of ideas or energy to produce change."* Don't allow your comfort zone to become your end zone.

It is time for all of us Kings-Priests and Priests-Kings to arise, shine, and transform the earth. Our time has come!

OTHER BOOKS BY DICK BERNAL

My Father Doesn't Own a Gas Station

Shaking Hands With God

Questions God Asks

Removing the "Ites" From Your Promised Land

Curses – What Are They and How to Break Them

Living Under An Open Heaven

The Laws of Seedtime & Harvest

One Hundred Life Lessons from a Jewish King

Who is God, What is Man

When Lucifer, Jezebel, or Jonah Join Your Team

To order these books or other books and teaching materials by the author, Dick Bernal, please visit our website at www.jubilee.org, or call Jubilee Christian Center's bookstore at 1-888-582-4533.